A CourseGuide for

Faith Alone

Thomas Schreiner

ZONDERVAN
ACADEMIC

ZONDERVAN ACADEMIC

A CourseGuide for Faith Alone

Copyright © 2020 by Zondervan

Requests for information should be addressed to:
Zondervan, *3900 Sparks Dr. SE, Grand Rapids, Michigan 49546*

ISBN 978-0-310-11052-1 (softcover)

CONTENTS

Introduction

Welcome to *A CourseGuide for Faith Alone*. These guides were created for formal and informal students alike who want to engage deeper in biblical, theological, or ministry studies. We hope this guide will provide an opportunity for you to grow not only in your understanding, but also in your faith.

How to Use This Guide

This guide is meant to be used in conjunction with the book *Faith Alone — The Doctrine of Justification* and its corresponding videos, *Faith Alone Video Lectures*. After you have read each chapter in the book and watched the accompanying video lesson, the materials in this guide will help you review and assess what you have learned. Application-oriented questions are included as well.

Each CourseGuide has been individually designed to best equip you in your studies, but in general, you can expect the following components. Most CourseGuides begin every chapter with a "You Should Know" section, which highlights key terminology, people, and facts to remember. This section serves as a helpful summary for directing your studies. Reflection questions, typically two to three per chapter, prompt you to summarize key points you've learned. Discussion questions invite you to an even deeper level of engagement. Finally, most chapters will end with a short quiz to test your retention. You can find the answer key to each quiz at the bottom of the page following it.

For Further Study

CourseGuides accompany books and videos from some of the world's top biblical and theological scholars. They may be used independently, or in small groups or classrooms, offering quality instruction to equip students for academic and ministry pursuits. If you would like to engage in further study with Zondervan's CourseGuides, the full lineup may be viewed online. After completing your studies with *A CourseGuide for Faith Alone*, we recommend moving on to *A CourseGuide for God's Word Alone* and *A CourseGuide for Christ Alone*.

CHAPTER 1

Sola Fide
in the Early Church

You Should Know

- Luke 23:39–43: "One of the criminals who hung there hurled insults at him: 'Aren't you the Messiah? Save yourself and us!' But the other criminal rebuked him. 'Don't you fear God,' he said, 'since you are under the same sentence? We are punished justly, for we are getting what our deeds deserve. But this man has done nothing wrong.' Then he said, 'Jesus, remember me when you come into your kingdom.' Jesus answered him, 'Truly I tell you, today you will be with me in paradise.'"

- When it comes to the notion that the church fathers were unanimous in their upholding the Roman Catholic view of justification, keep in mind they were not yet dealing extensively with that issue in their theological formulations. There is evidence among many church fathers that they did maintain justification by faith alone, but the church fathers are not always as clear on the subject as latter theologians would become.

- Imputed righteousness: being declared to be right before God on the basis of the righteousness of Jesus Christ, which is given to us when we believe

- Infused righteousness: being made righteous before God because of our righteous behavior, because of the righteousness that transforms and changes us

- Augustine: church father whose mature understanding of predestination led him into conflict with Pelagius over the role of faith and works in justification

- Forensic understanding of justification: being declared righteous before God

- Transformative understanding of justification: being made righteous before God

Essay Questions

Short

1. When studying the earliest Christians, should we expect them to have the same clarity on the issue of *sola fide* as the Reformers? Why or why not? How should they be read when considering this issue?

2. What is the difference between forensic understandings of justification and transformative understandings of justification?

3. Why is Augustine significant for understanding the history of the church's understanding of justification?

Long

1. If someone told you the Protestant doctrine of justification has no historical precedence beyond the sixteenth century, how would you respond? How would you answer the charge that the early fathers are unanimous in opposing justification by faith alone?

Quiz

1. (T/F) The church father Origen saw the thief on the cross's conversion as being in opposition to justification by faith.

2. (T/F) Those who affirm a Protestant view of justification and those who affirm a Roman Catholic view both appeal to Augustine for their views.

3. What pitfall do Protestants need to avoid when considering the history of the church?

a) Embracing theology that emerged before the sixteenth century
b) The true church only arose in the sixteenth century
c) Studying the writings of the earliest centuries of the church
d) Recognizing errors that have occurred in the past

4. When do we first encounter the beginning of a fuller discussion of the relationship between faith and works?

a) Augustine's dispute with Pelagius
b) Athanasius's dispute with Arius
c) Irenaeus's dispute with Valentinus
d) In the Didache

5. _____ righteousness means we are declared to be right before God on the basis of the righteousness of Jesus Christ, which is given to us when we believe. _____ means that we are righteous before God because of our righteous behavior, because of the righteousness that transforms and changes us.

a) Believer's, Christ's righteousness
b) Christ's, Believer's righteousness
c) Infused, Imputed
d) Imputed, Infused

6. "Good works" in Clement are:

a) The foundation for justification which continues to be honed through greater works of love
b) The appropriate response to the work of salvation, not the foundation of justification
c) The transformative grace that is gradually infused in the hearts of believers leading to an inherent righteousness
d) Unnecessary for believers to engage in if they have actually embraced Jesus Christ as their Savior

7. What aspect of Ignatius's discussion on justification sometimes leads to confusion on whether he held to justification by faith?

a) His appeal to his baptism
b) His beliefs about Mary
c) His emphasis on martyrdom
d) His discussion of gifts

8. The *Epistle to Diognetus* shows that _____ is not a modern notion.

   a) Infusion
   b) Faith
   c) Substitution
   d) Eschatology

9. Augustine understood the word "justify" to mean:

   a) Declare righteous
   b) Make righteous
   c) Begin salvation
   d) End righteousness

10. What doctrine especially influenced Augustine's view of justification?

   a) Sanctification
   b) Baptism
   c) Christology
   d) Predestination

CHAPTER 2

Martin Luther on Justification by Faith Alone

You Should Know

- Our righteousness is not grounded on faith, but faith is the means by which we lay hold of Christ. God is given all the glory if righteousness is grounded on Christ rather than faith.

- When it comes to the role for good works in the lives of believers, Luther saw good works as evidence of a genuine faith, and he saw all genuine obedience flowing from faith.

- Romans 3:28: "For we maintain that a person is justified by faith apart from the works of the law."

- *Simul iustus et peccator*: justified and at the same time sinners

- Part of the medieval understanding of righteousness: believers are made righteous in justification; God is faithful because he promises to save his people; God gives righteousness to those who believe in Jesus; and believers are rewarded by God based on their actions

- Luther's views of justification: God gave the law to show we could not attain justification through the law; works are a condition, but not a cause of salvation; the righteousness of Christ is an alien righteousness given to believers; justification is through faith alone in Christ alone

- Finnish interpretation of Luther: school of thought that sees participation with Christ and gaining attributes of his divine presence as central to the gospel

- Imputation: The righteousness of Christ is counted to believers and they are credited as being righteous even though they are not yet inherently righteous themselves

Essay Questions

Short

1. From Luther's perspective, what is the relationship between human sin and the law of God?

2. What is Luther's view of the imputation of Christ's righteousness? Why is there some confusion over what Luther believed about righteousness?

3. What did Luther mean by suggesting believers are "justified and at the same time sinners"?

Long

1. Martin Luther considered justification by faith alone the doctrine by which the church stands or falls. Do you agree with him? Why or why not? How can that statement be reconciled with the knowledge that there were no clear theological formulations dealing with justification by faith prior to the Reformation and Counter Reformation?

Quiz

1. (T/F) The dominant view of justification in the medieval period was that believers are *declared righteous*.

2. (T/F) Luther so emphasized the necessity of justification by faith alone that he did not see a need for good works in the lives of believers.

3. Which of the following is not one of the main three features in Lutheran and Protestant doctrines of justification?
    a) Justification is clearly distinguished from sanctification
    b) Justification denotes alien righteousness that is imputed to believers

   c) Justification provides a righteousness inherent to believers
   d) Justification is forensic rather than transformative

4. For Luther, what does freedom look like in the life of a sinner?

   a) They are ignorant of God and will not obey him until they learn of his existence
   b) Their wills are bent to do evil and all their works are wicked
   c) Their wills are free to do good or evil, but most people choose to do evil
   d) They are only capable of preparing themselves for grace; God must do the rest

5. What did Luther mean by saying our righteousness is passive?

   a) It is given as a free gift once we have genuinely worked for it
   b) We do not do anything to prepare for it or to receive it
   c) We received it in accordance with the amount of faith we have
   d) Christ gives it to those who are not actively engaged in worshiping other gods

6. In describing the imputation of Christ's righteousness to believers, what biblical metaphor does Luther appeal to in explaining imputation?

   a) The giving of talents to workers
   b) The marriage between Christ and the church
   c) The calling of laborers to work in the vineyard
   d) The drawing of water from a well

7. How does faith save believers?

   a) Faith is the means by which one lays hold of Christ, who is our righteousness
   b) Faith is the grounds of our justification through which we are considered righteous in Christ
   c) Faith, working with love, is the means by which we receive the righteousness needed to be justified
   d) Faith in Christ first provides engrafting into the covenant of God, but works accompany that allow one to remain in the covenant

8. What does simul iustus et peccator mean?

   a) Justified and at the same time without sin
   b) Justified and growing in holiness
   c) Justified and at the same time sinners
   d) Justified and growing in faith

9. What does the Finnish view of Luther's theology suggest?

   a) Justification is only a forensic declaration shifting our status before God
   b) Justification includes our participation in the divine nature
   c) Justification occurs for believers once they are raised from the dead
   d) Justification includes a new record, but the believer remains unchanged inherently

10. According to Dr. Schreiner, the Finnish view of Luther's theology bears similarity with what other doctrine?

   a) The Reformed doctrine of total depravity
   b) The Roman doctrine of absolution
   c) The Greek orthodox doctrine of *theosis*
   d) The Gnostic doctrine of *gnosis*

CHAPTER 3

John Calvin on Justification by Faith Alone

You Should Know

- Believers show their confession of faith to be genuine through good works. Believers are called to grow in holiness through the gift of sanctification. True saving faith expresses itself through love of God and neighbor.

- Calvin's views on justification: the righteousness of Christ is imputed to believers; justification is by faith alone as a gift given from God; union with Christ grants believers all the benefits of salvation including justification; and justification and sanctification are inseparable but must be distinguished

- Faith is an instrument that joins us to Christ. Faith is the means by which we receive the object of our faith, which is Christ and in him righteousness.

- Forensic: a legal view of justification where God declares someone to be in a right standing before him

- Union with Christ: doctrine advocated by Calvin that we are united to Christ by faith and receive every benefit of salvation in him

- Calvin's views on the place of good works in the lives of believers: Saving faith produces good works in the lives of believers; believers are not justified by good works but grow us in our fellowship with God; believers' righteousness is proved by the evidence of good works; and justification and sanctification can be distinguished but not separated

- Sanctification: the work of Christ in believers' lives whereby they are gradually made more and more like him

Essay Questions

Short

1. For Calvin, why is justification so important for understanding ourselves and God?

2. Does justification by faith alone nullify the importance of good works? Why or why not?

3. How is union with Christ important for understanding Calvin's doctrine of justification and sanctification?

Long

1. If someone suggested to you that the Protestant doctrine of justification by faith alone taught believers to not care about doing good works, how would you respond? What if they said they had seen it adversely impact an individual's faith? Utilize Scripture in your answer.

Quiz

1. (T/F) According to Calvin, believers cannot become more justified as they progress in holiness.

2. (T/F) According to Calvin, faith is our righteousness.

3. According to John Calvin, how does a sinner realize they cannot attain righteousness by their own works?
   a) By seeing themselves in comparison with others who are more righteous than they are
   b) By considering the continued effects of the fall throughout human history

c) By seeing themselves in light of God in his holiness

d) By considering whether the ceremonial laws continue today

4. In interpreting Paul, Calvin thought that works of the law referred to:

a) The entire law of God

b) Only the civil law

c) The law revealed in nature

d) Only the ceremonial law

5. What does Calvin see as characterizing true faith?

a) It is exercised once

b) It never suffers from doubt

c) It justifies on its own accord

d) It perseveres to the end

6. In Calvin's theology, from where do believers receive righteousness before God?

a) Through faith working in love

b) Through imputation of Christ's righteousness

c) Through imputation of a believer's righteousness

d) Through the infusion of grace

7. How does Calvin explain James 2:24–26 and its discussion of faith alone not justifying someone?

a) James is referring to proving our righteousness

b) James is referring to the imputation of Christ's righteousness

c) James is referring to holiness that results in justification before God

d) James is referring to examining one's faith in light of Christ

8. What metaphor does Calvin use to show justification and sanctification are inseparable but distinguishable?

a) The root and branches of a tree

b) The light and shifting of the tides from the moon

c) The fletching and head of an arrow

d) The light and warmth of the sun

9. How do believers receive justification and sanctification according to Calvin?

    a) Through faith in itself

    b) Through good works

    c) Through union with Christ

    d) Through love

10. For Calvin, we are justified:

    a) Without works

    b) Through works

    c) With, through, and by works

    d) Not without works yet not through works

CHAPTER 4

Sola Fide and the Council of Trent

You Should Know

- James 2:14: "What good is it, my brothers and sisters, if someone claims to have faith but has no deeds? Can such faith save them?"

- While Protestants deny the ground of good works for justification, they do believe they are still necessary in the lives of those who are already justified by faith alone in Christ alone.

- Regensburg Colloquy: the 1540s gathering between Protestants and Roman Catholics where they attempted to find unity

- The Council of Trent: the mid-1500s Roman Catholic council that responded to the Protestant critiques of the Roman Catholic church

- The big picture steps through which Trent believes justification occurs: God extends his grace to sinners through Christ; free will moves sinners to believe; believers exercise faith and works in cooperation with grace to be transformed; believers grow in their own righteousness

- Aspects of Trent's view of justification: the free will of human beings cooperates with God's grace; justification and merit are gained before God by virtue of works done by believers; the grace of justification can increase through good works; justification is not by faith alone in Christ alone

- Anathema: a declaration that someone will be deserving of eternal punishment if they maintain the doctrine that is under anathema

Essay Questions

Short

1. What were the responses of Calvin and Luther to the Regensburg Colloquy and why might they have responded as each did?

2. How did the Council of Trent misunderstand the Protestant doctrine of justification? Why do you think there was this misunderstanding?

3. Does Trent reject salvation by grace? Why or why not?

Long

1. Do you think there is a place today for further discussions between Catholics and Protestants concerning the doctrines that divide them? Why or why not? Based on your current understanding, what do you think are the core issues that divide them? How does justification play a part in that?

Quiz

1. (T/F) Calvin pursued unity with Rome until the day of his death.

2. (T/F) For the Council of Trent, justification is not limited to forgiveness of sins.

3. (T/F) The Council of Trent believed humans obtain God's grace through the exercise of their free will alone.

4. During the Reformation, the most significant attempt by Catholics and Protestants to find agreement on justification and other doctrines was the: (pg. 64)

   a) Marburg Colloquy
   b) Regensburg Colloquy
   c) Zurich Agreement
   d) Diet of Worms

5. Initially, the meeting between Protestants and Catholics before Trent found much agreement concerning _____ but ended because of discussions about _____ (pg. 64).

    a) The Trinity, justification

    b) Justification, the Trinity

    c) The church and the eucharist, justification

    d) Justification, the church and the eucharist

6. What was the significant text the Council of Trent appealed to in order to defend that faith cooperates with good works and increases our justification? (pg. 65)

    a) Romans 4

    b) James 2

    c) Galatians 5

    d) Jude

7. The Council of Trent declares justification is: (pg. 65)

    a) The final result of the intercession of Christ for believers

    b) A declaration given to Christ for his faithfulness

    c) A process that may increase or decrease in this life

    d) A once for all declaration from God given upon belief

8. What is the Council of Trent's position on assurance of salvation? (pg. 65)

    a) Everyone who is predestined can gain assurance of that truth

    b) No one can be sure they are among the predestined

    c) Those who engage in good works can be certain they are among the predestined

    d) Only clergymen can be sure they are among the predestined

9. According to Dr. Schreiner, how does the Council of Trent misunderstand the Protestant view of salvation? (pg. 65)

    a) Man cannot prepare himself to receive salvation

    b) Man can prepare himself to receive salvation

    c) Good works are necessary for believers

    d) Good works are unnecessary for believers

10. According to Dr. Schreiner, how does the Council of Trent properly understand the Protestant view of salvation? (pg. 65)
    a) Man cannot prepare himself to receive salvation
    b) Man can prepare himself to receive salvation
    c) Good works are necessary for believers
    d) Good works are unnecessary for believers

Glimpses into Further Discussions on *Sola Fide*: The Contribution of John Owen, Richard Baxter, and Francis Turretin

You Should Know

- Believers are given new life in addition to forgiveness and Christ's righteousness. Believers receive the gift of sanctification in addition to justification. Someone who claims to believe in Christ but does not follow his commandments to love God and neighbor are denying their faith.

- Philippians 3:8: "What is more, I consider everything a loss because of the surpassing worth of knowing Christ Jesus my Lord, for whose sake I have lost all things. I consider them garbage, that I may gain Christ."

- 1 Corinthians 1:30: "It is because of him that you are in Christ Jesus, who has become for us wisdom from God—that is, our righteousness, holiness and redemption."

- Covenant of redemption: eternal agreement between Father and Son to save his people

- Owen's views on justification: Christ's righteousness is imputed to believers and credited as their own; saving faith is not mere mental assent but one must trust and rely upon Christ; believers are justified by faith alone, but not by faith that is alone; faith is the instrument through which we receive Christ's righteousness

- Baxter's views on justification: believers have their sins forgiven, but do not have Christ's righteousness credited to them; faith is a believer's righteousness; the second justification is dependent on perseverance and grounded on imperfect works; justification is a lifelong process in the lives of believers

- Neonomian: "new law" or belief that second justification is grounded on obedience to God's commandments

- Antinomian: "against law" or belief that believers are free from any obligation to the law since they are justified by faith alone

Essay Questions

Short

1. Why and how does John Owen understand there to be a difference between intellectually affirming a doctrine versus actually believing it?

2. In Owen's thought, how does saving faith justify someone? How does Owen understand the relationship between faith and obedience as it relates to justification?

3. How is the idea of "covenant" important for Owen's understanding of imputation?

Long

1. Richard Baxter believed that the call to holiness in the lives of believers showed the necessity of an evangelical righteousness, which believers did not receive as imputed from Christ's righteousness. He viewed double imputation as leading to antinomianism or being against obedience to God's commandments. Do you think some of his concerns were valid? Why or why not? In what ways do you think his views may have misunderstood other positions on justification

by faith alone? Do you find anything compelling about his thoughts? Why or why not?

Quiz

1. (T/F) John Owen believed that Christ's passive obedience was credited to believers, but not his active obedience.

2. (T/F) According to Dr. Schreiner, Richard Baxter maintained that faith is our righteousness.

3. What belief of John Owen is an example of a catholic and charitable spirit?
   a) Everyone who professes to believe in Jesus Christ will be saved
   b) Roman Catholics and Protestants can agree to disagree while remaining Christians
   c) Some who do not believe in Jesus Christ will nevertheless be justified
   d) Some may be justified by faith alone even though they deny that doctrine

4. In Owen's theology, what kind of faith is necessary for salvation?
   a) Any faith worked from the heart that believes in God
   b) Mental assent to the truth in what God has revealed in his Word
   c) Knowledge of the gospel as revealed in God's Word
   d) Trusting in what God has revealed in his Word

5. Owen insists that perseverance in salvation is obtained by:
   a) Faith and works together
   b) Grace and man's will cooperating
   c) Works alone
   d) Faith alone

6. How does Owen understand James's use of the word "justify" in James 2?
   a) Believers are transformed for their justification
   b) Faith is proved to be true before people
   c) Faith is righteousness
   d) The believer is justified before God by faith alone

7. In Owen's view, what qualifies Christ as capable of acting as mediator?

   a) The satisfaction of Christ offered upon the cross at his crucifixion
   b) The high priestly prayer of Jesus given before his sacrifice
   c) The blending of God's love and justice
   d) The union of Christ's natures as planned from the covenant of redemption

8. What does it mean to reject double imputation but affirm single imputation?

   a) Believers receive Christ's righteousness as imputed to them, but forgiveness of sins only comes through perseverance in the faith
   b) Believers receive the forgiveness of sins as well as Christ's righteousness imputed to them
   c) Believers receive the forgiveness of sins, but Christ's righteousness is not imputed to them
   d) Believers receive faith as their righteousness, but cannot be forgiven of further sins after believing

9. What is Baxter's conception of fulfilling the law through evangelical righteousness known as?

   a) Antinomianism
   b) Neonomianism
   c) Socinianism
   d) Double imputation

10. According to Francis Turretin, love and works are _____ a person who is justified.

   a) Completed in
   b) Opposed to
   c) Required of
   d) Optional for

CHAPTER 6

The Status of *Sola Fide* in the Thought of Jonathan Edwards and John Wesley

You Should Know

- Some suggest Jonathan Edwards's views of justification are anti-Protestant. First, while Jonathan Edwards was often unclear, he nevertheless did affirm the Protestant views. Second, he affirmed justification is by faith alone. Finally, he maintained that Christ's righteousness is imputed to believers.

- Jonathan Edwards's views of justification: The righteousness of believers is grounded in imputed righteousness; good works are a necessary fruit of justification; genuine faith necessarily manifests itself as a persevering faith; justification is by faith alone

- John Wesley's views of justification: justification is by faith alone; Christ's righteousness is imputed to believers; good works are necessary as a fruit of salvation; imputation may not be used as an excuse for antinomianism

- Galatians 5:16: "So I say, walk by the Spirit, and you will not gratify the desires of the flesh."

- Single imputation: the view that Christ atones for sins but his righteousness is not credited to believers

- How Wesley's views on imputation seem to change over time: 1) He maintains single imputation; 2) he questions the use of "righteousness of Christ"; 3) he affirms the righteousness of Christ is imputed to believers; 4) he maintains Christ's righteousness is grounds of believers' righteousness but worries about antinomian misunderstandings of it.

- Inherent righteousness: the actual personal moral goodness of a person in relation to whether they themselves are righteous or not

Essay Questions

Short

1. What is Edwards's view on the relationship between faith and obedience? How can it be understood as orthodox for Edwards to suggest good works are necessary for salvation?

2. How does Edwards relate perseverance and justification?

3. Why does Dr. Schreiner think Wesley maintained justification by faith alone?

Long

1. Some have admired Jonathan Edwards's creativity when discussing the doctrines of the Christian faith. Others have found it confusing or unhelpful. Multiple and very different interpretations of his theology abound. Do you think there is a place for creative exercise when theologians think of and discuss established doctrines? Why or why not? What are ways Christians can maintain the riches of the church's history while exploring doctrine further? Is there even a way to do that? Explain.

Quiz

1. (T/F) Edwards saw that true faith always results in good works.

2. (T/F) When Edwards suggests good works are necessary for salvation, he sees works as a cause of justification.

3. (T/F) John Wesley maintained justification by faith alone.

4. Some people believe Jonathan Edwards's view on justification was close to:

- a) Arminianism
- b) Roman Catholicism
- c) Socinianism
- d) Eastern Orthodoxy

5. Even though he disagrees with the charges, which of the following is not a common charge against Edwards's view of justification?

- a) He saw a place for active righteousness in believers, not merely passive righteousness
- b) He misunderstood union with Christ in legal terms instead of personal communion
- c) He saw a place for double imputation upon believers who were united to Christ
- d) He saw a place for inherent righteousness, not only imputed righteousness

6. Edwards's understanding of "infused grace" is referring to:

- a) Regeneration
- b) Justification
- c) Inherent righteousness
- d) Sanctification

7. Edwards's discussion of faith and love should be interpreted as saying:

- a) Faith is the fruit of love
- b) Love is the fruit of faith
- c) Faith working with love justifies
- d) Faith is not as necessary as love

8. When Edwards seems to suggest that justification is progressive, he is rather declaring:

- a) Faith and obedience are inseparable
- b) Obedience must come first if one is to exercise their will to believe

c) Faith and love are one and the same

d) Obedience comes through hearing the Word of God

9. According to Dr. Schreiner, how does Edwards relate perseverance and faith?

a) Justification is grounded in perseverance

b) Perseverance is obtained by those who are inherently righteous

c) Perseverance flows from the first act of faith

d) Justification is declared whether one perseveres to the end or not

10. What was the most significant reason Dr. Schreiner suggests Wesley did not like using the language of imputation?

a) If misunderstood it could lead to antinomianism

b) It was in opposition to the Anglican understanding of justification

c) If taken to its logical conclusion it could lead to Roman Catholicism

d) It did not make sense to him

CHAPTER 7

Human Sin

You Should Know

- Some suggest the New Perspective on Paul is a proper reading of the apostle. However, Paul clearly teaches that when he was unconverted he was seeking to obey God's law to be righteous. Also, works of the law do not denote only boundary markers but all of God's law. Finally, works of the law refer to obedience required by God, and Paul advocates such obedience is impossible to make.

- Works of the Law: the term used by Paul to refer to obedience to all of God's law

- New Perspective on Paul: a view that Paul is not criticizing legalism among the Jews in his letters but their adherence to laws that separate Jews from Gentiles

- Reasons for why works of the law refer to the whole of God's law and not just the ethnic or ceremonial boundaries: Abraham was not justified by works prior to the giving of the Mosaic law; Paul accuses unbelieving Jews of moral failure; Paul says that everyone has sinned and falls short of the glory of God, including Jews; Paul says that a person is cursed if they do not do everything written in the law

- Respond to the charge that justification can come through works in this way: The law was given to show people could not fulfill the law; God is perfect and demands perfect obedience; Abraham was not justified by works but through faith

- Works: Paul's reference for the obedience required during the time of Abraham before the giving of the Mosaic law or general obedience

- Ephesians 2:8–10: "For it is by grace you have been saved, through faith — and this is not from yourselves, it is the gift of God — not by works, so that no one can boast. For we are God's handiwork, created in Christ Jesus to do good works, which God prepared in advance for us to do."

Essay Questions

Short

1. What is the New Perspective on Paul and the Roman Catholic understanding of "works of the law"? Why is this potentially problematic?

2. How does Paul use the words "works of the law" and works? Fundamentally for Paul, why are works not capable of justifying people?

3. How does Ephesians 2 help our understanding of justification by faith alone?

Long

1. How would you explain God's giving of the law? What purpose does it serve in God's plan of salvation? How would you explain it to a believer in your church?

Quiz

1. (T/F) Paul's reflection in Philippians 3 on his life of Judaism highlights that Paul thought he was only morally superior to others.

2. (T/F) According to Dr. Schreiner, God's grace is what God does, accomplishes, and gives to human beings.

3. Upon which biblical author have most of the justification debates been centered?

    a) Paul
    b) Peter
    c) John
    d) Moses

4. From the New Perspective understanding, as well as Roman Catholic, what does "works of the law" refer to when used by Paul?
   a) Civil law
   b) Moral law
   c) Ceremonial law
   d) The entire law

5. According to Dr. Schreiner, what does the term "works of the law" refer to?
   a) Civil law
   b) Moral law
   c) Ceremonial law
   d) The entire law

6. When Paul discusses the role of obedience in Abraham's life, why does he refer to "works" rather than "works of the law"?
   a) Abraham was faithful to works but not works of the law
   b) Abraham was not under the Mosaic law
   c) Abraham was justified by faith
   d) Abraham was never given a commandment he could not obey

7. What was Israel's calling as related to the pursuit of righteousness?
   a) They were to accomplish righteousness in the Mosaic law
   b) They were to put their faith in Jesus Christ
   c) They were to follow after the Davidic kings
   d) They were to show God's light to the Gentiles

8. According to Dr. Schreiner, why don't humans receive righteousness from works?
   a) God does not require perfection for obedience to works
   b) It was a ploy from Satan to suggest obedience from people would please God
   c) People are incapable of doing what the law commands
   d) Only those under the Old Covenant were capable of receiving it

9. When Paul reflected on his life in Judaism, what does he mean by saying he was "blameless"?
   a) His righteousness was extraordinary and he offered sacrifice when he sinned

b) He was not guilty of ordinary sins and offered sacrifices daily
c) He viewed himself as sinless through his conduct and zeal for the Torah
d) His life was marked by success in all of his endeavors and he prayed daily

10. In which Pauline text do we find a reflection of *sola fide*, *sola gratia*, *solus Christus*, and *soli Deo Gloria*?

a) Philippians 2:5–11
b) Romans 1:16–17
c) Ephesians 2:1–10
d) Galatians 3:15–18

CHAPTER 8

Faith Alone

You Should Know

- *Pisteuo*: Greek word meaning "believe"

- *Dikaioo*: Greek word meaning "justify"

- Examples of being saved by faith in Luke: the disreputable woman washing Jesus's feet; the healed Samaritan leper who returns to give glory to God; the blind man requesting Jesus open his eyes; the healing of the paralytic let in through the roof

- Examples of being saved by faith in Acts: the Gentile Cornelius and his household; the Philippian jailer and his household; the Ethiopian eunuch; Lydia the seller of purple cloth

- Respond to someone who said any form of faith in Christ is saving in this way: A bare faith that does not trust in Christ and manifests itself in good works is not a true faith; the parable of the sower shows that some initial responses to the gospel are not true faith.

- John 6:29: "Jesus answered, 'The work of God is this: to believe in the one he has sent.'"

- Simon Magus: magician in Acts who shows a false faith

Essay Questions

Short

1. How is "belief" in the Gospel of John focused on Christ and what are some of the ways he brings to light what faith in Christ looks like?

2. How does the Jerusalem Council in Acts 15 show that righteousness is not of works but rather faith?

3. For Paul, what is the nature of saving faith and how does it express itself in the lives of believers?

Long

1. Paul's letters are most common to consult when looking at the issue of justification by faith alone. However, what parts of the Gospels and Acts would you turn to in order to show and explain justification by faith alone? Provide at least ten specific examples and how these teach the doctrine of justification by faith alone.

Quiz

1. (T/F) Luke sometimes uses the phrase "*your faith* has saved you" when individuals believe in Jesus.

2. According to Dr. Thomas Schreiner, what is the difference between the Jewish leaders' perspective of the centurion and his own perspective of himself?

   a) The leaders thought he was unworthy to receive Jesus, but he saw himself as worthy
   b) The leaders thought Jesus should not waste time on a Gentile, while he believed he could appeal to Jesus
   c) The leaders thought he was worthy to receive Jesus, but he saw himself as unworthy
   d) The leaders thought he was worthy to receive Jesus, and he saw himself as worthy

3. Given the absence of the word "faith" in the parable of the Pharisee and the tax collector, what is there to suggest, then, justification by faith alone?

   a) The tax collector left "justified" solely through God's mercy
   b) The Pharisee left "justified" through his reliance upon the God of Abraham

    c) The tax collector left "justified" by the work of penance and contrition

    d) The Pharisee and the tax collector left "justified" by the same God

4. How does the Gospel of John show the centrality of belief?

    a) The children of God are all those made in God's image

    b) Faith produces miraculous works in the lives of all believers

    c) Those who disbelieve will receive a second chance at faith

    d) Only those who believe will enjoy life in the age to come

    e) All of the above

    f) None of the above

5. When Jesus feeds the five thousand in John 6, what do they seek from him?

    a) To understand who they are to place their faith in

    b) To arrest him and make him cease from talking

    c) To know what good works they must do

    d) To know why their nation has been conquered

6. What designation given to Christians in Acts shows the fundamental importance of faith?

    a) Christians

    b) Followers of the way

    c) Saints

    d) Believers

7. What individual in Acts shows there is such a thing as false faith?

    a) Mark

    b) Simon Magus

    c) Timothy

    d) Festus

8. What happens to those who do not believe in the gospel?

    a) They are given a second chance to believe

    b) They will not receive as much of a reward as those who do believe

    c) They will face eschatological humiliation

    d) Nothing

9. According to Dr. Schreiner, what makes faith salvific?

    a) The object of faith
    b) The subject of faith
    c) The strength of faith
    d) The age of faith

10. Faith that is real:

    a) Is exercised once
    b) Cannot be weak
    c) Ends at death
    d) Leads to works

CHAPTER 9

Faith in Jesus Christ

You Should Know

- *Pistis Iesou Christou*: woodenly translated from the Greek — faith of Jesus Christ

- Objective genitive: the genitive is the object of the action of the first noun

- Subjective genitive: the genitive is the subject of the action of the first noun

- Arguments in support of *pistis Iesou Christou* being translated as "faithfulness of Christ" or as subjective genitive: it is superfluous for Paul to speak of faith in Christ with nouns when he previously uses a verbal clause to describe faith in Christ; faithfulness of Jesus fits with and is another way of speaking of Jesus's obedience that achieved salvation; it accords with Paul's theology that God's work is accomplished by the faithfulness of Jesus and not the human response of faith; in Romans 4:12 the phrase refers to the "faith of our father, Abraham," and so the phrase in other instances should be rendered as "faithfulness of Jesus"

- Arguments in support of *pistis Iesou Christou* being translated as "faith in Christ" or as an objective genitive: Paul uses faith in Christ with a variety of expressions and we cannot straitjacket his usage; Paul nowhere else, outside of disputed passages, uses faith or faithful to describe Jesus's obedience; the nouns saying faith in Christ are not superfluous when mixed with the verbal clause but rather is a matter of emphasis; the genitive object with "faith" is very clear in some instances

- Examples of faith in Christ in other texts: Ephesians 1:15, "I heard about your faith in the Lord Jesus"; Colossians 1:4, "We have heard of your faith in Christ Jesus"; Philemon 5, "I hear about your love [. . .] and your faith in the Lord Jesus"; Colossians 2:5, "How firm your faith in Christ is."

- Galatians 2:16a: "Know that a person is not justified by the works of the law, but by faith in Jesus Christ."

- Galatians 2:20: "I have been crucified with Christ and I no longer live, but Christ lives in me. The life I now live in the body, I live by faith in the Son of God, who loved me and gave himself for me."

Essay Questions

Short

1. What is the subjective genitive understanding of *pistis Iesou Christou*? (pg. 126–127)

2. What is the objective genitive understanding of *pistis Iesou Christou*? (pg. 128–129)

3. Why is the debate over *pistis Iesou Christou* important?

Long

1. Based on your current understanding of the issue, how do you think *pistis Iesou Christou* should be translated? Why? If the opposite was actually true, would it affect your understanding of justification? Why or why not?

Quiz

1. (T/F) If *pistis Iesou Christou* "faith of Jesus Christ" refers to "faithfulness of Jesus Christ," then righteousness by faith is not true.

2. (T/F) Paul uses a variety of expressions to describe faith in Christ and we must take care to not straightjacket his usages.

3. (T/F) Throughout the entire argument of Romans 3 and 4 Paul is describing the faith of Christ.

4. Translating *pistis Iesou Christou* as "the faithfulness of Jesus Christ" is what kind of genitive?

    a) Source
    b) Absolute
    c) Subjective
    d) Objective

5. Proponents of "faithfulness of Jesus Christ" suggest it would be _____ for it to be "faith in Jesus Christ" if it follows after the verbal clause "belief in Jesus Christ."

    a) Precise
    b) Redundant
    c) Epexegetical
    d) Subjective

6. Translating *pistis Iesou Christou* as "faith in Jesus Christ" is what kind of genitive?

    a) Source
    b) Absolute
    c) Subjective
    d) Objective

7. As it relates to genitive constructions, what is a clear example of a genitive being used objectively to speak of Christ?

    a) Knowing Christ Jesus
    b) Knowledge possessed by Christ Jesus
    c) Wisdom from Christ Jesus
    d) Faithfulness of Abraham

8. According to Dr. Schreiner, why might Paul use a verbal construction of belief in Christ and immediately follow it with a noun construction to express faith in Christ?

    a) To clarify
    b) For ease of reading
    c) For emphasis
    d) It is arbitrary

9. Outside of the disputed texts referring to *pistis Iesou Christou*, where else do we find references to "faith" or "faithful" in relation to Christ's obedience?

    a) The synoptic Gospels
    b) A few texts in Romans and Philippians
    c) Throughout Galatians
    d) Nowhere

10. Some opponents of "faith in Christ" claim that emphasizing faith in Christ is:

    a) Pelagian
    b) Hyper-Calvinistic
    c) Socinian
    d) Amyraldian

CHAPTER 10

The Importance of Justification in Paul

You Should Know

- Justification deals with the issue of how sinful humans can hope to stand in the presence of a holy and just God, which is accomplished through faith alone in Jesus Christ alone. While it is not primarily ecclesiological, it does affect our view of our standing before God and how all other people relate to one another within the church in light of this truth.

- Arguments that suggest justification is not the center of Paul's theology include: the term righteousness predominately only appears in polemical letters; Paul's theology can be explained without discussing justification; and justification was a means to an end for Paul to include the Gentiles in the church

- Douglas Campbell: a theologian who advocates that justification theory is an improper understanding of Paul

- 1 Thessalonians 1:9: "For they themselves report what kind of reception you gave us. They tell how you turned to God from idols to serve the living and true God."

- Romans 4:6–8: "David says the same thing when he speaks of the blessedness of the one to whom God credits righteousness apart from works: 'Blessed are those whose transgressions are forgiven, whose sins are covered. Blessed is the one whose sin the Lord will never count against them.'"

- Passages that allude to justification by faith alone even if they do not use the terms righteousness or justification necessarily:

1 Thessalonians 1:9, where the Thessalonians turned to God from idols; 1 Thessalonians 5:9, where God did not appoint his people to wrath but they have obtained salvation through Jesus; Romans 4:6–8, where David is credited with righteousness and it is explained in terms of forgiveness of sins; Romans 6, where those who have died with Christ have been raised with him

- Polemical theology: theology given in response to difficulties, attacks, or problems within the church

Essay Questions

Short

1. What is the place and importance of justification in Christian doctrine?

2. How are there ecclesiological and ethical ramifications to justification by faith alone?

3. How do the two letters to the Thessalonians show Paul's concern for justification?

Long

1. Do you think there is a theological "center" or "pillar" for understanding all of Scripture as the most significant doctrine? Why or why not? Whether you do or not, what, based on your current understanding of Scripture, do you think are the most significant doctrines and why? [This next qualifier might make the question too long] How do they relate to one another?

Quiz

1. (T/F) According to Dr. Schreiner, justification is at the center of Paul's theology.

2. (T/F) Whenever Paul turns to what God has done for believers in Jesus Christ, he only rarely includes justification.

3. N. T. Wright suggests that justification is fundamentally _____ instead of _____.

    a) Ethical, legal

    b) Legal, ethical

    c) Ecclesiological, soteriological

    d) Soteriological, ecclesiological

4. Why did Paul proclaim justification by faith?

    a) So Gentiles might be included as God's people

    b) For pragmatic purposes

    c) To defeat his opponents

    d) It is the truth

5. According to Dr. Schreiner, what would happen if Paul's polemical theology was restricted?

    a) We would not have much of his theology left

    b) We would not understand his opponents

    c) We would find the center of his theology

    d) We would see the importance of justification

6. The very meaning of the word "justification" is _____.

    a) Soteriological

    b) Ecclesiological

    c) Forgiveness

    d) Redemption

7. If Paul brings in justification as an antidote to pride, then:

    a) Justification has only forensic implications

    b) Justification relates to ethics

    c) Justification is synonymous with sanctification

    d) Justification is the center of Christianity

8. Second Thessalonians does not address justification directly, but it has many uses from the:

    a) "Righteousness" word group

    b) "Loving" word group

    c) "Faith" word group

    d) "Perseverance" word group

9. _____ is the grounds of _____.

    a) Justification, sanctification
    b) Sanctification, justification
    c) Salvation, resurrection
    d) Resurrection, salvation

10. Douglas Campbell claims that Romans 1:18–32 represents:

    a) Paul's views
    b) Paul's opponents' views
    c) Jesus's views
    d) Christian views

CHAPTER 11

God's Saving Righteousness

You Should Know

- Genesis 15:6: "Abram believed the Lord, and he credited it to him as righteousness."

- *Sidqot*: Hebrew word for "righteous acts" or "saving acts"

- *Sedaqa*: Hebrew word for "righteousness"

- Examples of righteousness following a norm: Judah declaring Tamar to be in more of the right than he was; Jacob saying he was honest before Laban; Saul, while seeking to kill David, affirms David is more righteous than he is; weights for the economy were to be accorded to a certain standard

- Righteousness: a norm according to God's standards

- Examples of God's righteousness including his judgment: the judgment brought upon Sodom and Gomorrah; the Lord promises to repay every person for "his righteousness"; God is depicted as a judge throughout Scripture; Israel's exile was just punishment for their apostasy

- Covenant faithfulness: N. T. Wright's definition of righteousness, that God is faithful to his covenant

Essay Questions

Short

1. What do the Hebrew words *sidqot* and *sedaqa* mean and what do they teach about righteousness?

2. What is the relationship between righteousness and covenant?

3. How is righteousness seen in terms of God's salvation? How is righteousness seen in terms of God's judgment?

Long

1. Dr. Schreiner explains that discussions of God's righteousness must include salvation and judgment. Why is it important for the Christian faith to embrace the knowledge that God is both just and merciful? How could this knowledge help in apologetics to unbelievers?

Quiz

1. (T/F) According to Dr. Schreiner, righteousness and salvation are equivalent words.

2. (T/F) According to Dr. Schreiner, righteousness should not be defined as covenant faithfulness.

3. (T/F) According to Dr. Schreiner, righteousness is limited to God's salvation.

4. The Hebrew word *sidqot* can be translated as
   a) Faithfulness or love
   b) Justice or holiness
   c) Presiding acts
   d) Righteous acts or saving acts

5. In Genesis 15:6, where Abraham's faith is counted as righteousness, it means:
   a) He has done the ethically right thing to do
   b) He is counted as standing in the right before God
   c) He has engaged in a saving act for his nephew Lot
   d) He is considered glorified before God

6. Given the extensive presence of _____, righteousness in the Old Testament is often depicted as forensic (pg. 147).

a) Courtroom imagery
b) Harvesting imagery
c) Worshiping imagery
d) Marriage imagery

7. The covenant promises of God are:

a) Unrelated to descriptions of God's saving righteousness
b) The only means by which God's righteousness is made manifest
c) Another way of describing God's saving righteousness
d) Only fulfilled through Old Testament deliverances

8. God's saving righteousness _____ the covenant.

a) Is
b) Fulfills
c) Transforms
d) Becomes

9. According to Dr. Schreiner, righteousness refers to:

a) Covenant faithfulness
b) A norm according to a standard
c) Unswerving allegiance to God's glory
d) Faith

10. What is the standard for righteousness?

a) The conditions for salvation
b) Cultural covenants
c) The age in which righteousness is practiced
d) God's own character

CHAPTER 12

Righteousness Is Eschatological

You Should Know

- The order of believers' justification in relation to Christ's justification: 1) Christ's perfect obedience in his life; 2) Christ's death upon the cross; 3) Christ's resurrection as his vindication; 4) believers receive Christ's vindication and are justified through faith; 5) believers are openly acquitted on the final day of judgment

- Jesus's resurrection: the moment when Jesus was vindicated

- 1 Timothy 3:16: "Beyond all question, the mystery from which true godliness springs is great: He appeared in the flesh, was vindicated by the Spirit, was seen by angels, was preached among the nations, was believed on in the world, was taken up in glory."

- Examples of justification seeming to be done in the "past": Romans 4:2, "If, in fact, Abraham was justified by works"; Romans 5:1, "Since we have been justified through faith"; 1 Corinthians 6:11, "But you were washed, you were sanctified, you were justified in the name of the Lord Jesus Christ and by the Spirit of our God"; 1 Timothy 3:16, "[Jesus] was vindicated by the Spirit."

- Examples of justification seeming to be done in the "future": Romans 2:13, "Those who obey the law [. . .] will be declared righteous"; Galatians 2:17, "But if, in seeking to be justified in Christ, we Jews find ourselves also among the sinners"; Romans 8:33, "It is God who justifies"; Galatians 5:5, "For through the Spirit we eagerly await by faith the righteousness for which we hope."

- Examples of justification seeming to be vague on when it occurs: Romans 3:20, "No one will be declared righteous in God's sight by the works of the law"; Romans 3:26, "So as to be just and the one who justifies those who have faith in Jesus"; Galatians 3:24, "the law was our guardian until Christ came that we might be justified by faith"; Galatians 5:4, "You who are trying to be justified by the law have been alienated from Christ."

- Eschatology: the doctrine of the last things

Essay Questions

Short

1. What does it mean to say justification is eschatological?

2. What is the significance of Jesus's resurrection as it relates to justification?

3. How can justification be both future and past?

Long

1. Some have critiqued that speaking eschatologically (already/not yet) of justification would lead one to believe in two different justifications for believers. Do you think this is a valid criticism? Why or why not? Do you think there is truth in it? Why or why not? How would you explain it to a believer who maintained the Protestant view of justification by faith alone but had never thought of justification as an already/not yet concept? What Scriptures would you use?

Quiz

1. (T/F) The future justification of believers is revealed and announced in the present for those who believe in Jesus Christ.

2. (T/F) Believers might doubt their justification because they cannot know if they are justified in this life.

3. Which of the following passages suggest justification is in the future?

   a) "Since we have been declared righteous by faith"

   b) "For through the Spirit, by faith, we eagerly wait for the hope of righteousness"

   c) Jesus "was vindicated by the Spirit"

   d) "And those He called, He also justified; and those He justified, He also glorified"

4. Which of the following passages suggest justification is in the past?

   a) "But if we ourselves are also found to be 'sinners' while seeking to be justified by Christ"

   b) "The doers of the law will be declared righteous"

   c) "But you were washed, you were sanctified, you were justified in the name of the Lord Jesus Christ and by the Spirit of our God"

   d) "For through the Spirit, by faith, we eagerly wait for the hope of righteousness"

5. Which of the following passages are vague about the time of justification?

   a) "So that He would be righteous and declare righteous the one who has faith in Jesus."

   b) "You who are trying to be justified by the law are alienated from Christ"

   c) "He made the One who did not know sin to be sin for us, so that we might become the righteousness of God in Him."

   d) "But if we ourselves are also found to be 'sinners' while seeking to be justified by Christ"

   e) A & B

   f) C & D

6. According to Dr. Schreiner, when does the declaration as to who is acquitted and who is condemned occur?

   a) The day of judgment

   b) The day of a person's birth

c) The day of a person's death

d) The day a person is converted

7. According to Dr. Schreiner, when was Jesus "justified"?

a) His birth

b) His resurrection

c) His ascension

d) His death

8. Why might believers enjoy justification at present?

a) Believers enjoy the fruits of their Spirit-wrought works which leads to justification

b) Believers are united to Christ by faith and he was vindicated by his resurrection

c) Believers experience the resurrection of their bodies now through union to the risen Christ

d) Believers notice their failings and sins but continue to persevere in spite of them

9. What aspect of future justification do believers look forward to?

a) Their attaining to being inherently righteous

b) The possession of Christ's righteousness

c) The public declaration that they are justified

d) The assurance of salvation

10. What is a significant problem for Roman Catholicism when they deny assurance of salvation?

a) They fail to see the end-time verdict has been declared in advance

b) They fail to remain consistent with their views of inherent righteousness

c) They fail to hold the tension of God's justice and mercy in balance

d) They fail to recognize the need for one to have faith

ANSWER KEY

1. T, 2. F, 3. B, 4. C, 5. E, 6. A, 7. B, 8. B, 9. C, 10. A

CHAPTER 13

Righteousness Is Forensic

You Should Know

- Believers are declared righteous because they are given the righteousness of Jesus Christ imputed to them, rather than being gradually transformed until they are fully justified. Justification is the basis for sanctification and, thus, all those who are justified will certainly be sanctified, but the two must be distinguished.

- The divine courtroom includes God having the ability to actually give the perfect righteousness of his Son to believers, but even when this is given to them, they themselves are not inherently righteous.

- Arguments in support of seeing justification as transformative: the righteousness of God in Romans 1:17 is transformative because it parallels the power of God in Romans 1:16; God's righteousness is revealed or manifested, thus it is a power that changes humans; through Christ's obedience the many are *made* righteous because of Christ; justification includes both the death and resurrection of Christ which includes not only forgiveness but also new life

- Arguments in support of seeing justification as forensic: the proceedings in a courtroom enact a declarative judgment, not a transformative one; Job already thinks he is not guilty so he wants God to declare him to be righteous, not transform him; the prophets prosecute Israel and say God's righteous judgment will come upon them; a judge does not make someone righteous

- The work of a judge in a courtroom: they declare someone guilty; they declare someone innocent; they make declarations in accordance with a set standard; they weigh whether the person did or did not act righteously

- Romans 8:33: "Who will bring any charge against those whom God has chosen? It is God who justifies."

- Romans 6:7: "Because anyone who has died has been set free from sin."

- *Logizomai*: Greek word meaning "credited" or "counted"

Essay Questions

Short

1. What are the strongest arguments that Paul's view of righteousness is transformative?

2. How does the prevalent language of a courtroom contribute to our understanding of righteousness?

3. How does the relationship between faith and righteousness point towards a forensic understanding of righteousness?

Long

1. The Bible is full of courtroom imagery and Paul discusses justification through many of his epistles. Nevertheless, many find the emphasis on the legal aspects is at times either overdone or not warranted by Scripture. Thus, the emphasis is often on the transformation aspects. Do you think there is too much of an emphasis made by the church on the forensic aspects of the Christian faith? Why or why not?

Quiz

1. (T/F) A transformative reading doesn't necessarily contradict the Reformation if the transformative is the basis for the forensic.

2. (T/F) If the law were kept, justification would be gained by works of the law, but even in this instance, they would still be *declared* righteous rather than *made* righteous.

3. Why does Dr. Schreiner think the Old Testament is significant for determining Paul's view on righteousness?
   a) Paul spent most of his time debating fellow Jews
   b) It was Paul's Bible
   c) Paul supplemented his thinking with it
   d) It was the only source of revelation

4. Which of the following is not an argument supporting righteousness as referring to transformation?
   a) If one man's disobedience made many unrighteous, then one man's obedience makes them righteous
   b) God's righteousness is revealed showing it is not merely a gift but also a power
   c) Anyone who has died has been set free from sin
   d) Man is credited as righteous apart from works

5. Righteous judges do not:
   a) Advise on matters of righteousness, they model them
   b) Model matters of righteousness, they advise on them
   c) Make persons guilty or innocent, they declare them to be
   d) Declare persons guilty or innocent, they make them to be

6. What is Job seeking from God in his misery?
   a) To be lifted up from the ashes and restored to his former life
   b) To have a court case before God in order to be declared right
   c) To receive the transformation of God's presence and no longer be evil
   d) To hear words of sympathy from godly friends

7. Why cannot Romans 8:33 mean "make righteous"? Text reference: "Who will bring any charge against those whom God has chosen? It is God who justifies."
   a) This is one of the few places where it is clear that righteousness is transformative, but since it is speaking of a courtroom setting it cannot be "make righteous"

b) It is contrasted with "accusation" and it does not follow that God makes someone wicked on the last day

c) It is contrasted with the many things that cannot separate believers from the love of God in Christ

d) It is placed within the context of "righteous" living

8. How can believers be counted righteous if they have not done righteous deeds?

a) They will one day have the necessary righteousness

b) They are united to Jesus by faith

c) They do not need to have righteousness

d) They are placed in an estate where they can accrue righteousness

9. In which passage does Dr. Schreiner concede that most see "justify" having a transformative meaning, even though he does not believe it compromises that the majority of the cases are forensic?

a) Romans 3:21: "But now apart from the law the righteousness of God has been made known"

b) Galatians 5:5: "For through the Spirit we eagerly await by faith the righteousness for which we hope"

c) Romans 6:7: "Because anyone who has died has been *set free* from sin"

d) Romans 5:1: "Since we have been *justified* through faith"

10. Why do some think "the ministry of righteousness" in 2 Corinthians 3:8 is referring to transformation?

a) It is paralleled with the sanctifying work of the Spirit

b) It is speaking of believers growing in righteousness

c) It is contrasted with condemnation that the wicked receive

d) It is given in the context of the Mosaic Covenant

CHAPTER 14

The Righteousness of God

You Should Know

- Philippians 3:9: "And be found in him, not having a righteousness of my own that comes from the law, but that which is through faith in Christ — the righteousness that comes from God on the basis of faith."

- When God makes a verdict of righteous, it is true that the person is righteous in his eyes; it is not a legal fiction, but their righteousness is not their own but rather Christ's imputed to them.

- This does not include the transformative element which does come from sanctification, but is restricted to the verdict that God has made upon those who have Christ's righteousness.

- Romans 10:2: "For I can testify about them that they are zealous for God, but their zeal is not based on knowledge."

- Examples that suggest the righteousness of God is a gift he can give: Philippians 3:9 explicitly says that Christ's righteousness comes from God through faith; the contrast between Adam and Christ suggests Christ's righteousness comes as a gift as the many are made righteous in him; in 1 Corinthians 1:30, Paul says that believers are given wisdom, sanctification, redemption, *and righteousness*; Romans 3:21–24 points to righteousness being given through faith and it is related to the righteousness of God

- The Righteousness of God: an attribute of God and something he can gift to believers

- Genitive of source: the genitive is the source from which the noun derives or depends

- Genitive of description: the genitive describes what the noun is characterized by

Essay Questions

Short

1. What does it mean to say "God's righteousness" is an attribute of God? Why is it important to acknowledge "judgment" as part of God's righteousness?

2. How can righteousness be said to be a gift from God?

3. How can God's righteousness be said to be effective without compromising justification by faith alone?

Long

1. The righteous requirements of the law flow from God's own perfect righteousness. Righteousness is an attribute of God, but, according to Dr. Schreiner, it is also a gift he bestows on those who believe in Jesus Christ. How is understanding God's own righteousness helpful for these discussions about justification? What are some other doctrinal examples where the implications or gifts to believers are rooted in God's own attributes?

Quiz

1. (T/F) Luther's understanding of justification turned on his comprehension that the "righteousness of God" in Romans 1:17 meant acquiring a right standing before God.

2. (T/F) According to Dr. Schreiner, the fact that most of the uses of "righteousness of God" does not include the preposition "from" should lead one to question whether righteousness is indeed a gift.

3. (T/F) Words associated with righteousness are too often used to define righteousness.

4. According to Dr. Schreiner, the righteousness of God is:

    a) Genitive of source

    b) Genitive of description

    c) Partitive genitive

    d) Genitive of apposition

    e) A & B

    f) C & D

5. If righteousness is by faith, then the righteousness of God is also a:

    a) Reward

    b) Wage

    c) Gift

    d) Merit

6. How would one's own righteousness be acquired without faith in Christ?

    a) By perfectly fulfilling the mandates of the law

    b) By striving to fulfill the mandates of the law

    c) By faithful obedience and confession of sin

    d) By discovering God's will in his Scriptures

7. What is the relationship between Paul when he was unconverted and unbelieving Israel?

    a) Both sought to obtain God's favor through faith in Christ

    b) Both sought to establish their own righteousness by observing the law

    c) Both were examples of Old Testament righteousness

    d) Neither believed that YHWH was God

8. Romans 5:19, where it is often translated being "made" righteous, is probably better translated as:

    a) Blessed

    b) Infused

    c) Appointed

    d) Born

9. Peter Leithart argues that God's judgment is:

   a) Perfected through the perfecting of believers
   b) A forensic declaration
   c) Not only a legal verdict but also effective and executive
   d) Only a legal verdict

10. How can we say that God's verdict, as it relates to righteousness, is effective?

   a) Sinners who trust in Christ are truly righteous before God, but it is not their righteousness
   b) Sinners who trust in Christ are truly righteous before God because they are transformed unto righteousness
   c) Sinners who trust in Christ are given a legal verdict but also delivered into a new state of existence
   d) Sinners who trust in Christ are given a legal verdict and inherently made perfect by that verdict

CHAPTER 15

Imputation of Righteousness

You Should Know

- Examples of arguments against imputation: a judge does not give his righteousness to a defendant; First Corinthians 1:30 must also include imputation of wisdom, sanctification, and redemption; Second Corinthians 5:21 says we become God's righteousness, rather than it being credited to us; the most natural way to read of righteousness in Romans 4:1–8 suggests faith is our righteousness

- Examples of arguments for imputation: the larger context of Romans 5:12–19 suggests when we are united to Christ we receive all that he is and has done for believers; what saves believers is not ultimately their faith but the object of their faith; Second Corinthians 5:21 says we become God's righteousness because it is imputed to us; First Corinthians 1:30 says we receive different gifts of God all in Christ but not necessarily in the same exact way

- 2 Corinthians 5:21: "God made him who had no sin to be sin for us, so that in him we might become the righteousness of God."

- Galatians 3:6: "So also Abraham believed God, and it was credited to him as righteousness."

- Faith is an instrument by which believers receive the object of their faith, Jesus Christ, who is their righteousness. Faith cannot be said to save in and of itself; rather, it receives Christ.

- True and genuine saving faith shows it possesses Christ's righteousness through the doing of good works. Believers receive Christ's righteousness and are justified in him, but they also receive the newness of life in him and walk by his Spirit.

- N. T. Wright: a renowned contemporary scholar who maintains the New Perspective on Paul and denies imputation of Christ's righteousness
- Active obedience of Christ: the actual fulfilling of the law by Christ which is credited to believers in imputation as though they had fully kept the law

Essay Questions

Short

1. Why do N. T. Wright and Robert Gundry deny the imputation of Christ's righteousness to believers?

2. How does the contrast made between Adam and Christ by Paul help us in our understanding of imputation?

3. How does faith justify someone?

Long

1. A common objection to Christ dying for our sins and us receiving his righteousness is the claim that such a doctrine is tantamount to cosmic child abuse. Islam maintains that a person cannot have their sins atoned for by another; rather, they must stand before Allah in their own righteousness. How would you respond to these charges and also use it as an opportunity to magnify the gospel?

Quiz

1. (T/F) The language of active and passive obedience, while potentially helpful, is not necessary when affirming the imputation of Christ's righteousness.

2. (T/F) Given the centrality of the cross in Paul's theology, faith is the righteousness of believers.

3. Why does N. T. Wright deny the imputation of Christ's righteousness?

   a) He actually affirms the imputation of Christ's righteousness
   b) He argues a judge cannot declare someone to be righteous; he can only affirm a proven verdict
   c) He argues that justification is not a matter of declaring someone to be righteous; rather, it is the gifting of new life
   d) He argues a judge can declare someone to be righteous, but they do not give their righteousness to the person

4. Which of the following is not a reason that Robert Gundry argues against the imputation of Christ's righteousness?

   a) Christ's righteousness cannot be imputed to believers on account of Adam being the federal head of humanity
   b) Texts supporting the imputation of Christ's righteousness speak of God's righteousness being given to us, not Christ's
   c) The one righteous act of Christ that grants justification is his work on the cross, not his lifelong obedience
   d) Any discussions of faith being counted to believers as righteousness most naturally means that faith is our righteousness

5. Why can't the obedience of Jesus's whole life be separated from his obedience at the cross?

   a) It would not be possible for believers to know how to live properly if Christ had not shown it
   b) Obedience is a matter of life and does not include the actual act of sacrifice
   c) His death on the cross would not avail us if he were not obedient in all of life
   d) The entirety of his life is not what is imputed to believers, but the expiation of sin from death on the cross

6. What do the New Testament writers emphasize that Jesus obeyed?

   a) The Torah
   b) The law of God
   c) The customs of the Old Testament
   d) The will of the Father

7. How does faith save believers?

   a) It is the righteousness of believers
   b) It is an instrument that connects humans to Christ
   c) It fulfills the commandments of the law
   d) It is the object of our salvation

8. In 2 Corinthians 5:21, how could the word "become" mean "becoming" and still teach the imputation of Christ's righteousness?

   a) Believers gain a right standing before God through union with Christ when they were previously condemned
   b) Believers become righteous through the transformation of their faith as received by Christ's faith
   c) Believers acquire the means through which to embrace the gifts of God's mercy
   d) Believers change from one degree of glory to the next when they are finally justified in Christ

9. According to Dr. Schreiner, what is the most challenging objection to the claim that 1 Corinthians 1:30, which speaks of those in Christ receiving wisdom, righteousness, sanctification, and redemption from God, is proof for imputation?

   a) One would have to affirm we have received adoption, regeneration, and illumination from God as well
   b) Those gifts are said to only be given to Paul and the other workers of the gospel
   c) One would have to affirm that wisdom, sanctification, and redemption are also imputed
   d) It is referring to receiving all of these things from God rather than from Christ

10. Why is it improper to object that a judge cannot give righteousness to someone?

   a) God is not a judge but rather a Father who delights to forgive his fallen creatures
   b) God is able to forgive sinners through Christ, something a human court cannot do

c) A person in court can receive another person's condemnation if they volunteer to receive it instead

d) A judge is able to do whatever he wants to do within the courtroom that he presides over

CHAPTER 16

The Role of Good Works in Justification

You Should Know

- James 2:19: "You believe that there is one God. Good! Even the demons believe that—and shudder."

- James is not critiquing justification by faith; rather, he is critiquing a bare faith that is not a true faith. True saving faith trusts in Christ and is not only an agreement to historical facts; rather, it will manifest itself through works.

- Paul believes that those who sow to the flesh will receive condemnation. Paul believes justification is by faith alone, but he also says those who are justified will produce the fruit of the Spirit and if they do not, they are showing themselves to be still in darkness.

- Paul and James are dealing with two different issues but are in agreement with one another. Paul is combating those who would follow legalism and be justified by works of the law, while James is dealing with antinomians who would use faith as a cover to not obey God and live unto righteousness.

- Galatians 5:21b: "I warn you, as I did before, that those who live like this will not inherit the kingdom of God."

- Examples of a living and active faith: faith obeys Jesus and to not believe in him is to be disobedient; caring for other believers is given divine reward; those who love Jesus are also those who keep his commandments; believers who possess faith are also marked by putting to death the works of the flesh and producing fruits of the Spirit

- James says God demands perfection (James 2:10) and says we all sin regularly (3:2), so he cannot be in opposition to justification by faith alone. If justification came through works of the law, then James would be contradicting himself by acknowledging that God demands perfection but humans cannot attain it.

- James was dealing with antinomian perceptions of faith and thus was making charges against a deficient faith that could not save. Bare faith is not enough to save, for even demons possess that kind of faith; rather, saving faith expresses itself in love and fulfilling of the royal law of God.

- Faith for James is shown to be genuine and justifying through the producing of good works. Actual saving faith manifests itself in good works.

- Bare faith: a mere mental agreement or assent to facts but does not place trust in them

Essay Questions

Short

1. What does deficient faith look like in Matthew and John? (pg. 194–195)

2. What is Paul's perspective on the necessity of good works?

3. How can Paul and James be reconciled in their views of justification?

Long

1. According to Dr. Schreiner, it is necessary to affirm both justification by faith alone as well as the necessity of good works for final justification. Do you agree that it is proper to use this language? Why or why not? What are some of the challenges you perceive (or have seen) that could flow from saying good works are necessary for salvation?

Quiz

1. (T/F) For John, believing in Jesus is contrasted with disobedience.

2. (T/F) According to Dr. Schreiner, obedience to God isn't motivated by a desire to be accepted by God.

3. What is a bare faith?
   a) Faith that is the bare sufficiency for attaining to justification through union with Jesus
   b) Faith that complicates love because it does not understand the fullness of the gospel
   c) Faith that perpetuates simple views about Jesus but is still able to justify
   d) Faith that subscribes to mental propositions but doesn't embrace and love Jesus

4. What parable does Matthew describe that shows persevering faith is necessary?
   a) Parable of the wandering sheep
   b) Parable of the workers in the vineyard
   c) Parable of the hidden treasure
   d) Parable of the sower

5. While miraculous signs are given to evoke belief, what is a danger they can engender as shown in John's Gospel?
   a) One can fail to be the recipient of them if they are not witnessed
   b) One can be driven to worship if they see a sign
   c) One can be tempted to seek after power that will enable them to do such miracles
   d) One can be entranced by signs and fail to see what the signs point to

6. Who are examples in Paul's life and ministry of those who have a dead faith?
   a) Luke and Epaphroditus
   b) Demas and Hymenaeus
   c) Timothy and Titus
   d) Peter and Barnabas

7. What kind of faith would not be recognized by John?

   a) Faith that pursues the object of its affection
   b) Faith that justifies
   c) Faith that is separated from activity
   d) Faith that leads to obedience

8. What is the contrast being made with the parable of building a house on rock versus sand in Matthew?

   a) Those who do not hear and those who do hear
   b) Those who hear and obey versus those who only hear
   c) Those who attempt to obey without hearing and those who obey after hearing
   d) Those who obey and those who believe

9. Justification in James means:

   a) Make righteous
   b) Prove to be righteous
   c) Declare righteous
   d) Infused with righteousness

10. How does Dr. Schreiner think James is using justification by works?

   a) Works function as evidence of the reality of faith
   b) Works are the basis for one's justification
   c) Works transform towards justification
   d) Works are unnecessary for life, but they are helpful

CHAPTER 17

Sola Fide and the Roman Catholic Church

You Should Know

- Merit: a reward or recompense accrued from God's grace and attained through man's collaboration

- Imparted righteousness: the view that righteousness is infused into believers and is transforming them through justification

- The Joint Declaration of the Doctrine of Justification: the meeting between Lutheran World Federation and the Roman Catholic Church to come to an agreement on justification

- Evangelicals and Catholics Together: a document formed by several Protestants and Catholics in an attempt to find common ground on social issues

- Examples that highlight the Roman Catholic view of righteousness: baptism is part of the process that justifies believers; Christ's righteousness is imputed to believers and it grows in them; justification is a lifelong process for a believer; in cooperation with God's grace, believers can merit eternal life and temporal goods

- Rome has not changed its position on Trent's definition of justification. Rome, even if it does not want to use the anathemas, still maintains that justification is a process that involves meritorious efforts of believers.

- Evangelicals believe justification is a declarative act, while Rome views it as an ongoing process. These two positions are completely antithetical to one another and posit two different views of salvation.

- Order of the Roman Catholic view of justification which includes the sacraments: 1) God provides a way of salvation in his incarnate Son; 2) human beings choose with their own free will God's grace offered to them; 3) baptism washes the person of original sin; 4) good works are performed to accrue merit alongside confession, penance, and mass

- Richard Neuhaus: a Lutheran who was converted to Roman Catholicism and played a leading role for the Catholic side in ECT

Essay Questions

Short

1. Summarize the Catholic Catechism's view of justification.

2. What was the purpose and intentions of the Joint Declaration of the Doctrine of Justification? What aspects of the Joint Declaration are problematic as it relates to justification?

3. What was the purpose and intentions of Evangelicals and Catholics Together? What affirmations made by Evangelicals and Catholics Together are problematic as it relates to justification?

Long

1. In a global context where Christianity has spread around the whole world and is faced with a myriad of challenges to the faith, many bodies of believers are seeking greater unity in the face of these challenges. Do you think there is a way to seek unity and cooperation on social issues between different branches of Christianity? Can the doctrines that have divided us be maintained while also still seeking to love one's neighbor or is compromise on those doctrines necessary? Why or why not?

Quiz

1. (T/F) Neuhaus's fundamental argument in favor of unity between Rome and Protestants is that justification by faith alone is not an important doctrine.

2. The Catholic Catechism defines justification as:

   a) Declaring righteous
   b) Making righteous
   c) Glorification
   d) Faith

3. What is the place of merit for the Catholic Catechism?

   a) Initial grace cannot be merited, but through the Spirit people can merit the graces needed for eternal life
   b) Initial grace is merited through choosing to be baptized, and subsequent merit is given through the Spirit
   c) Initial grace is merited through faith, but through the Spirit people acquire further grace by the practice of good works
   d) There is no place for merit in the Roman Catholic view of salvation

4. Protestants believe in _____ righteousness, but Catholics in _____ righteousness.

   a) Everlasting, temporal
   b) Temporal, everlasting
   c) Imputed, imparted
   d) Imparted, imputed

5. What document arose out of a meeting between the Lutheran World Federation and the Roman Catholic Pontifical Council for Promoting Christian Unity in the late 90s?

   a) Evangelicals and Catholics Together
   b) Affirmations and Denials Concerning the Doctrine of Justification
   c) Joint Declaration of the Doctrine of Justification
   d) Decrees Seeking to Bring Unity Between Protestants and Rome

6. According to Dr. Schreiner, what is a fundamental problem with many ecumenical documents?

   a) There is too much division to warrant their creation
   b) They are seeking unity

c) They are too detailed

d) They are too ambiguous

7. What document sparked controversy when several well-known Protestant and Roman Catholic voices met with one another in order to promote cooperation on social issues?

a) Evangelicals and Catholics Together

b) Affirmations and Denials Concerning the Doctrine of Justification

c) Joint Declaration of the Doctrine of Justification

d) Decrees Seeking to Bring Unity Between Protestants and Rome

8. Which of the following was not an objection to Evangelicals and Catholics Together?

a) rConversion is defined in Catholic terms as a life-long process instead of a decisive moment when one believes

b) Concessions are made to Lutheran understandings that Roman Catholics and Reformed both deny

c) It seems the statement discourages evangelism among Roman Catholics

d) Identifying Roman Catholics as fellow believers is disingenuous since they deny the gospel and most are not believers

9. Why does Dr. Schreiner believe appealing to Augustine as the source of Roman Catholic and evangelical understandings of justification and thus a means of unity between them is wrongheaded?

a) Augustine's theology is influential to Roman Catholics but not evangelicals

b) Nothing has changed between Rome and Protestants as it relates to their appeals to Augustine

c) It has been 1,600 years since Augustine and there is more clarity on the issue now

d) Everyone who has followed Augustine's view of justification has invariably maintained a wrong view of the sacraments

10. What was Richard John Neuhaus before he converted to Roman Catholicism?

- a) Lutheran
- b) Reformed
- c) Anglican
- d) Methodist

CHAPTER 18

Frank Beckwith's Return to Rome

You Should Know

- Hebrews 11:8: "By faith Abraham, when called to go to a place he would later receive as his inheritance, obeyed and went, even though he did not know where he was going."

- Examples of Frank Beckwith's arguments in favor of Catholicism: the early church fathers did not maintain the Protestant view of justification; Scripture shows that people will receive eternal life based on what they have done; justification is a cooperation between the human will and God's grace; sanctification is included in justification

- Assurance is rooted in Christ when believers receive all that he is through faith alone. Among the gifts given to believers is justification whereby they know that if they believe in Jesus Christ then they are justified before God.

- Good works encourage assurance and strengthen it, but are not the grounds of it. Explanation: Believers are called to walk in obedience to Christ and if they are living a life contrary to it, ought to not have a strong assurance, but the ultimate assurance of any believer is that they believe in Jesus Christ alone for their salvation.

- Works cannot be the basis of our standing before God because he requires perfection, something no sinful human can achieve. Explanation: The only way for people to be righteous before God is if they believe in Jesus Christ and receive his righteousness imputed to them through faith.

- The works which are presented on the final day of judgment are evidence that we were always justified by faith. Explanation: God has prepared those whom he saves by grace alone through faith alone to do good works and he gives new life to those whom he justifies so that they live sanctified lives as well, but their works are not the grounds of their justification.

- Frank Beckwith: a scholar who was raised Roman Catholic, converted to Protestantism, and then later in life returned to Roman Catholicism

- Catholic view of assurance: can only be granted by direct special revelation from God

- Nominalism: a philosophy that teaches there are not essences but only names

Essay Questions

Short

1. What and why does Beckwith think is the plain reading of Scripture as it relates to good works?

2. Why does Beckwith believe justification is a process? How does Beckwith conflate justification and sanctification and why is this problematic?

3. Contrast the Roman Catholic view of assurance of salvation with the Protestant view.

Long

1. From Dr. Frank Beckwith's perspective, Protestants and Roman Catholics share effectively similar views of assurance of salvation. How would you explain to a Roman Catholic the Protestant view of assurance of salvation? How would you then actually apply that doctrine to those who are struggling with assurance as Protestants?

Quiz

1. (T/F) Discussions about justification are too often marred by accusations of name-calling and heresy hunting.

2. (T/F) Genesis 15:6 is the first time Abraham was justified.

3. From a Roman Catholic perspective, where is the issue of justification by faith alone discussed in the Bible?

   a) Romans 3:28 and it is vague on the relationship between faith and works
   b) 1 John 2:15 and it suggests those who are believers will not sin
   c) James 2:24 and it expressly denies justification by faith alone
   d) Galatians 3:10 and it says only those who follow the ceremonial law are condemned

4. What was Dr. Frank Beckwith's spiritual journey? (pg. 232–233)

   a) Evangelical to Roman Catholic to Eastern Orthodox
   b) Roman Catholic to Evangelical to Eastern Orthodox
   c) Evangelical to Roman Catholic back to Evangelical
   d) Roman Catholic to Evangelical back to Roman Catholic

5. Beckwith believes the early church fathers clearly did not espouse what particular doctrine that Protestants maintain? (pg. 233)

   a) Imputation
   b) Infusion
   c) Hypostatic union
   d) Final justification

6. Beckwith maintains that the clearest reading of the New Testament suggests that people: (pg. 234)

   a) Receive eternal life based on what they have done
   b) Evidence their justification through good works
   c) Are justified in this life through faith
   d) Are saved only through grace and apart from works

7. Why does Beckwith suggest Genesis 15:6 cannot be the moment Abraham was first justified?

a) Abraham is credited as finally justified at the sacrifice of Isaac in Genesis 22
b) Abraham had already followed God by faith as early as Genesis 12
c) Abraham does not manifest the fruit of his faith until he is circumcised in Genesis 17
d) Abraham is not deemed righteous until after his passing in Genesis 25

8. Beckwith believes good works don't _____, but they _____.

a) Justify the ungodly, sanctify the righteous
b) Sanctify the righteous, justify the ungodly
c) Get you into heaven, get heaven into you
d) Get heaven into you, get you into heaven

9. Paul says work out your _____, but never says work out your _____.

e) Salvation, justification
f) Justification, salvation
g) Salvation, sanctification
h) Sanctification, salvation

10. How does the Roman Catholic Church believe assurance of salvation comes to a believer?

a) Only through baptism
b) Only after sufficient works of penance are performed
c) Only through special revelation from God
d) Only when one is nearing the end of life

CHAPTER 19

N. T. Wright and the New Perspective on Paul

You Should Know

- Examples give support for the soteriological character of justification: Paul discusses works of the law, regardless of its meaning, to denote *how* one is not right with God; justification language is regularly linked with other soteriological terms and expressions; Romans 10:10 says, "For it is with your heart that you believe and are justified, and it is with your mouth that you profess your faith and are saved"; justification discusses how one becomes right with God with ecclesiological implications coming from having been made right with God

- 2 Corinthians 3:9: "If the ministry that brought condemnation was glorious, how much more glorious is the ministry that brings righteousness!"

- In Galatians, Paul is indeed dealing with the issue of whether Gentiles become circumcised, but the heart of the issue is that his opponents believe they should be circumcised because they need to obey the law to be justified. Paul and his Judaizing opponents were not on the same page for how someone is saved; rather, his opponents believed keeping the law justified a person or made them right before God.

- Ecclesiology: the doctrine of the church

- Boundary markers: N. T. Wright's view of how the works of the law were used by Jews to keep out Gentiles

- E. P. Sanders: the original scholar who brought the New Perspective on Paul to the forefront

- Titus 3:5: "He saved us, not because of righteous things we had done, but because of his mercy. He saved us through the washing of rebirth and renewal by the Holy Spirit."

Essay Questions

Short

1. Briefly summarize N. T. Wright's view of justification.

2. Why does Wright view justification primarily as ecclesiological?

3. Why is it better to see justification as primarily soteriological with implications for other doctrines?

Long

1. Wright has been very helpful in showing people how to read the Bible as a whole narrative rather than looking at it piecemeal. It is beyond the scope to detail the whole theological narrative of Scripture, but how would you at least summarize the doctrine of justification as it is shown throughout the big picture narrative of Old and New Testament?

Quiz

1. (T/F) Dr. Schreiner believes that N. T. Wright is correct to suggest that the New Testament Jews saw themselves as still living in exile.

2. (T/F) Wright maintains that perfection is necessary for believers to be found just in the final eschatological judgment.

3. Who launched "the New Perspective on Paul" into the academic world?
   a) James D. G. Dunn
   b) E. P. Sanders

c) N. T. Wright
d) John Barclay

4. N. T. Wright views justification as:

    a) Transformative
    b) Perfection
    c) Optional
    d) Forensic

5. Wright overemphasizes justification as primarily being:

    a) Soteriological
    b) Ecclesiological
    c) Eschatological
    d) Christological

6. Forgiveness of sins and justification are fundamentally:

    a) Soteriological
    b) Ecclesiological
    c) The same
    d) Different

7. What does Wright suggest is the fundamental problem in Galatians?

    a) How do people come into relationship with God?
    b) Who is one allowed to eat with?
    c) How is one justified before a holy God?
    d) When will the last days occur?

8. Why were the opponents in Galatians requiring Gentiles to be circumcised?

    a) They sought to make everyone Jewish
    b) They believed Gentiles would replace them
    c) They viewed circumcision as necessary for salvation
    d) They wanted to spare the Gentiles from persecution

9. What was the fundamental sin of the Jews?

    a) They excluded Gentiles from the people of God
    b) They ignored the Sabbath

c) They ceased offering sacrifices to God
d) They failed to obey God and keep his law

10. In Titus 3:5, which says "works done in righteousness" do not save us, how is this evidence against Wright's view of "works of the law"?

a) They are works done "in righteousness"
b) Paul is speaking to a primarily Jewish audience
c) Titus would not have understood the ceremonial law
d) Merit is not spoken of in this passage

CHAPTER 20

New Perspective on Paul: The Sin of Israel and the Rejection of Imputation

You Should Know

- 1 Corinthians 1:2a: "To the church of God in Corinth, to those sanctified in Christ Jesus and called to be his holy people."

- Israel's fundamental problem was they became idolaters who refused to obey God's law. While the name of God was blasphemed among Gentiles because of Israel's sin, they were punished by God for sinning against him.

- Israel had become like the nations and thus acted against God's law. The principle relationship that Israel ended up having with the nations was one of becoming idolatrous like them and brought upon exile.

- A human courtroom is a metaphor of the divine courtroom but does not encapsulate the whole of God's courtroom. God uses many metaphors from our experiences in creation and all of creation teaches something about him and his glory, but the finite cannot contain the infinite God.

- A human judge cannot give his righteousness to someone, but Christ is able to give his righteousness to those who believe in him. It is not possible for a human judge to give his righteousness to someone, but God in Christ is not under such a restriction, for those who are united to Christ by faith do actually receive his righteousness as credited to them.

- Christ's crediting of his righteousness to God's people is not a play on words, as they actually possess Christ's righteousness even though they themselves are not righteous yet. Believers actually are united to Christ and receive his righteousness and they also receive new life and sanctification, so that they gradually grow in their own personal holiness even as they are credited as fully righteous on account of Christ.

- Deuteronomy 25:1: "When people have a dispute, they are to take it to court and the judges will decide the case, acquitting the innocent and condemning the guilty."

- Definitive sanctification: doctrine that we are holy before God based on what Christ has done for us

- Progressive sanctification: doctrine that God is progressively increasing our own personal holiness by his grace as we put to death sin and pursue the fruits of the Spirit

Essay Questions

Short

1. What is N. T. Wright's understanding of Israel's problem and why is this problematic according to Dr. Schreiner?

2. What is problematic with Wright's interpretations of 1 Corinthians 1:30 and 2 Corinthians 5:21 according to Dr. Schreiner?

3. Why is union with Christ important for understanding imputation?

Long

1. Dr. Schreiner quotes Martin Luther speaking of believers possessing a righteousness that is not visible as they have it by faith; it is not theirs but it is Christ's perfect and eternal righteousness. What

difficulties are before believers living in this world, as they have to live by faith rather than by sight? Does the doctrine of justification by faith alone afford comfort through those circumstances? Why or why not?

Quiz

1. (T/F) Part of God's plan in giving the law to Israel was to reveal to them and the whole world the law could be kept.

2. (T/F) Wright believes 2 Corinthians 5:21, "God made him who had no sin to be sin for us, so that in him we might become the righteousness of God," should be restricted to Paul.

3. (T/F) According to Dr. Schreiner, Wright makes the mistake of assuming a human courtroom functions exactly the same as a divine courtroom.

4. What is the overall focus of the prophets when they rebuke Israel?
   a) Israel's idolatry and failure to follow God
   b) Israel's failure to bless the nations of the earth
   c) Israel's adherence to the Torah and Davidic throne
   d) Israel's tolerance for Gentiles

5. Wright suggests the common Protestant understanding of Israel's relationship to the law is guilty of suggesting:
   a) God has a plan A of salvation and then shifted to plan B
   b) The law was meant to be obeyed by Israel
   c) God's judgment rests upon the sinful and fallible hearts of men
   d) The giving of the law was the primary means of salvation

6. Wright suggests that justification _____ the status of a vindicated person by a/an _____.
   a) Declares, creation
   b) Creates, declaration
   c) Infuses, atonement
   d) Atones, infusion

7. Why is imputation vitally necessary for believers?

   a) God requires perfect obedience to be justified
   b) Inherent righteousness must be attained in this life
   c) It enables one to receive the infused righteousness of Christ
   d) He does not argue that it is necessary

8. When Paul says we have received wisdom, righteousness, sanctification, and adoption from God (1 Corinthians 1:30), what is sanctification referring to?

   a) Gradual sanctification
   b) Glorified sanctification
   c) Definitive sanctification
   d) Progressive sanctification

9. How does Wright view the legal declaration of justification?

   a) It is not based on one's moral character
   b) It is based on one's moral character
   c) It is determined based on one's obedience to the law
   d) It is determined based on the personality of the judge

10. What do believers receive when they are united to Christ?

   a) Righteousness
   b) Justification
   c) Sanctification
   d) All of who Christ is

CHAPTER 21

A Concluding Word

You Should Know

- Romans 10:17: "Consequently, faith comes from hearing the message, and the message is heard through the word about Christ."

- The essential elements of saving faith, in the proper order:
  1) knowledge; 2) assent; 3) trust

- Knowledge of our sin and knowledge of Christ as the answer to our sin is necessary. We need to know what is the truth of our own estate before the holy God, as well as to know that he has sent his Son as the one who can save us from our sins.

- With the knowledge of Christ, we are also to intellectually assent to the truth of that knowledge. It is not enough to receive the knowledge that we need Christ, but we also need to assent or agree to that.

- As we intellectually assent to Christ, we are to trust, embrace, and lean on him alone for our justification. Intellectual assent alone, however, is not satisfactory, as even demons agree that Jesus is the Son of God and Messiah. True faith fully embraces Jesus and trusts that he is who he says he is and he has accomplished what he says he has accomplished.

- 1 Corinthians 15:10a: "But by the grace of God I am what I am, and his grace to me was not without effect."

- The church's history is filled with many sins and failures, but that does not deny the truth of Christ's work for all who believe in him. It cannot be denied that the church has been guilty of many sins, but the truth of Christ is not invalidated by its conduct, even if it is hurt in the eyes of others.

- Christ has also worked powerfully through the church from the moment he ascended and is continuing to work powerfully through it. While the church has been guilty of sin, it also is the instrument through which God advances his purposes and brings people into his kingdom.

- The church this side of heaven is like the people within its midst, simultaneously justified and still sinful. The church is made up of the people of God who all are justified but are also still sinners warring against their sinful natures by the power of the Spirit. A blessed state of existence Christ promises to whomever believes in him.

- Hebrews 7:22: "Because of this oath, Jesus has become the guarantor of a better covenant."

Essay Questions

Short

1. What is necessary for saving faith?

2. Why isn't faith our righteousness?

3. How is the Christian experience proof of the comfort of justification by faith alone? How is the church's experience proof of the comfort of justification by faith alone?

Long

1. Is the doctrine of justification by faith alone something you believe and find comfort in? Why or why not?

Quiz

1. (T/F) According to Dr. Schreiner, because faith rests on Jesus we are not responsible for persevering in our faith.

2. (T/F) Our righteousness, even after we are Christians, can't qualify us to enter the new creation and God's presence.

3. (T/F) The church has been faithful throughout its history since the apostles.

4. What happens if mental assent is lacking in faith?

   a) It will save but not sanctify
   b) It cannot save
   c) The process of salvation is beginning
   d) One will only increase in faith afterwards

5. What is required beyond mental assent?

   a) Trust
   b) Knowledge
   c) Affirmation
   d) Nothing

6. According to Dr. Schreiner, why does faith save?

   a) It is a believer's righteousness
   b) Its object is Jesus Christ
   c) It sanctifies believers
   d) Its subject is believers

7. Through Jesus Christ, we receive:

   a) Justification
   b) New life
   c) The Holy Spirit
   d) Sanctification
   e) A & B
   f) C & D
   g) All of the above

8. Those who are justified in this life:

   a) Continue to sin
   b) Cease to sin
   c) Are glorified
   d) Overcome all temptations

9. What is our hope for life anchored in?

    a) Our achievements

    b) Our righteousness

    c) God's grace in Christ

    d) Our sanctification

10. What does Dr. Schreiner conclude is the end of justification by faith alone?

    a) People's salvation

    b) The renewal of the earth

    c) The transformation of the church

    d) God's glory alone

ANSWER KEY:

1. F, 2. T, 3. F, 4. B, 5. A, 6. B, 7. G, 8. A, 9. C, 10. D

Notes

www.ingramcontent.com/pod-product-compliance
Lightning Source LLC
Chambersburg PA
CBHW010920040426
42445CB00017B/1927